jB   12-906088
GRAF

                          10.95

Monroe, Judy
   Steffi Graf

jB   906088
GRAF

                          10.95

Monroe, Judy
   Steffi Graf

Steffi Graf

By
Judy Monroe

CRESTWOOD HOUSE

Mankato, Minnesota
U.S.A.

LIBRARY OF CONGRESS CATALOGING IN PUBLICATION DATA

Monroe, Judy
  Steffi Graf
  SUMMARY: A biography of the West German tennis player who won her first Grand Slam tournament at age seventeen and received the number one ranking in 1987.
  1. Graf, Stephanie, 1969-   —Juvenile literature. 2. Tennis players—Germany (West)—Biography—Juvenile literature. [1. Graf, Stephanie, 1969- . 2. Tennis players.] I. Title. II. Series.
GV994.G7M66   1988   796.342'092'4—dc19   87-30115
ISBN 0-89686-368-9

International Standard Book Number: 0-89686-368-9	Library of Congress Catalog Card Number: 87-30115

PHOTO CREDITS

Cover: Globe Photos, Inc: (S. Gelberg)
Focus West: (William Hart) 4, 11, 21, 24-25, 39; (T. Friedman) 23
Globe Photos, Inc.: 7, 9, 12, 15, 16, 29, 36-37
Sports Illustrated: (Frank Micelotti) 8, 34-35; (Manny Millan) 30-31, 32-33, 44-45, 46-47
Reuter/Bettman: 26, 28
Advantage International: 42
AP/Wide World Photos: (Paul Burnett) 18, 41; (Adam Stoltman) 40

CRESTWOOD HOUSE
Hwy. 66 South Box 3427
Mankato, MN 56002-3427

TABLE
OF
CONTENTS

Steffi Graf began playing tennis when she was four years old.

"I WANT TO HIT THE BALL"

Every evening, young Steffi Graf greeted her work-weary father with the same plea. "Play with me, Papa," she begged, a tennis racquet at her feet. "I want to hit the ball."

Finally, her father sawed the handle off an old tennis racquet and gave it to his daughter. Although not yet four years old, Steffi had enough wrist strength to firmly grasp the handle.

First, she tried hitting a ball over a row of chairs in the living room. Within a few days, she had damaged a lot of furniture! Next, she strung a string between two chairs in the basement. With her father offering instructions, Steffi began playing tennis.

Stephanie Graf was born on June 14, 1969, in Bruehl, West Germany. This town of 15,000 people is near Heidelberg and about one hour from the large city of Stuttgart.

Both of Steffi's parents played tennis. Her father, Peter, had begun playing at age 27 and earned a national ranking two years later. With the help of his wife, Heidi, he operated a tennis facility, giving tennis lessons after working hours.

Steffi's parents quickly recognized her talent. Her father noticed many eight-year-olds who were not as good as Steffi at age four. "Unlike the other children, she didn't hit the ball and then look all around at other things," he later remembered. She was always watching the ball until it was not in play anymore. Nothing distracted her."

"I was never someone who *watched* tennis," declared Steffi—she wanted to play! She began to learn basic tennis strokes: forehand, backhand, and volley. She learned how to serve or put the ball into play.

Steffi also learned the rules of tennis, one of the few games that is played around the world under the same rules. In tennis, a game is won by at least two points. A set consists of a player winning at least six games. The winner of a match must win two out of three sets.

In 1974, at five years old, Steffi moved her practice area from the basement onto a tennis court. She won her first junior tournament in Munich the very next year!

The following year, Mr. Graf quit his businesses and built a small tennis club to nurture Steffi's talents. Although Mrs. Graf had suffered a back problem and no longer played tennis, she began accompanying Steffi to tennis tournaments.

TURNING PRO

With her steady practice and father's coaching, Steffi rapidly improved. The legendary Billie Jean King admired Steffi's early playing. "What I liked when I first saw her as a 12-year-old was her footwork and discipline." At 13, Steffi competed in the West German Junior Championship and won.

That year, she made a major decision. She turned pro, earning money for her tennis playing. At the age of 13 years

When Steffi was 13 years old, she was ranked No. 12 in West Germany.

and 4 months, Steffi became the second youngest player to receive a ranking in the Women's International Tennis Association (WITA), No. 214. On the West German adult list, she ranked No. 12.

Steffi with her No. 1 coach—her dad!

She dropped out of school, but continued home studies with a tutor. Her father encouraged Steffi to develop concentration skills, and often played memory games with her.

For one game, called "Animals," Mr. Graf said, "I would recite the alphabet, and Steffi would stop me at a letter. Then she had to write as many animals as she could that began with that letter." For the letter S alone, Steffi could remember 100 animal names! Her ability to memorize whole pages of text for school exams helped Steffi in tennis. "One of my best things," she emphasized, "is to always be there, mentally."

Concentration is an important part of Steffi's game.

A NEW DREAM

Steffi began playing—and winning—in the international junior tennis circuit, and by the end of 1983, she had moved up to No. 98 in the WITA rankings. But in 1984, Steffi dreamed of another challenge. She wanted to win an Olympic gold medal. With her father continuing as her coach, she practiced hard.

The 1984 Olympic Tennis Demonstration was held in early August, at the new Los Angeles Tennis Center. Although tennis won't become an official medal sport until the 1988 Games in Seoul, South Korea, all competitors played with an Olympic spirit.

Steffi was 15 and the youngest player in the tournament. The fans loved her exciting matches. Her outstanding forehand shots and good timing made her unbeatable. She won and received the women's gold.

Later, she said, "I thought I'd come far because I was in good shape. I hoped to come as far as possible, but I didn't think I'd win. It was an unbelievable feeling!"

By early 1985, Steffi ranked No. 22 in women's international tennis. She had shown that she could play and win consistently. But she was still new to the world of championship tennis, and she wasn't always used to losing. During several tournaments, she cried on the court and acted rudely to sponsors and fans.

In one televised tournament, Steffi lost to Martina Navratilova, who was ranked No. 1 at that time. Steffi became upset and left the court in a hurry before the

Where will the ball land?

traditional presentation of prize money to the winner. Both the audience and the tournament officials thought this was poor sportsmanship.

Two weeks later, WITA officials met with Steffi and her father. They advised Steffi that she needed to learn to be more mature on the court. It would be better for her and better for the popularity of the sport. Steffi promised she would behave better.

A CLOSE MATCH

In early September 1985, Steffi made headlines during the U.S. Open tournament in New York. Gaining the quarterfinals, she upset top-ranked Pam Shriver in three crackling tie-breaker sets, winning $168,212 in prize money.

Tennis fans and officials roared at her solid passing shots and excellent forehand, the weapon of every champion.

Afterwards, Steffi said, "In the first tiebreaker, Pam was up 3-0 and serving, and I thought this set was lost, but I won it! Then the next set I was up 4-1 in the tiebreaker, and lost. Finally, in the third set I was 4-1 down and again I won it!

"It was a really good match," she continued, "and either one of us could have won. I don't think I've ever played such an unbelievably close match."

Time for a quick break before heading back onto the court.

A NEW COACHING RULE

Because Steffi works hard, Mr. Graf finds it easy to coach his extraordinary daughter. "Normally I'm very aggressive," admitted Mr. Graf. "Most fathers push their children very hard, but I don't push Steffi because she's very disciplined.

"I spend most of my time telling her to slow down," he explained. "Sometimes, I have to say 'Stop' because she works so hard. I have to tell her to relax, because she's very critical of her game."

Both Steffi and her father are aware of the feared "burnout" that has ruined other young tennis stars. Because of that, Mr. Graf limits Steffi to a maximum of 16 tournaments each year.

To further guard against burnout, Mr. Graf instituted a new rule for Steffi. Late in 1985, while ranked as the women's No. 10 tennis player, she took a three-and-a-half month break from matches and tournaments.

She practiced making her serve more effective and adding strength and variety to her backhand stroke. Her powerful forehand was already feared by opponents. Even a great player like Chris Evert Lloyd admitted being "intimidated" by it.

Steffi worked on her concentration. She sometimes let a close call by a referee distract her. This tended to make her game uneven.

Steffi also rested. "My father is always telling me to take it easy and relax, but it's difficult for me.

"The time I took off was an important thing for me," she said. "The only hard part was having to take off two weeks without touching a racquet. I always begged my father to let me hit the ball a little, but he insisted I rest."

In 1985, Steffi took a break from tennis to rest and practice.

STEFFI'S FIRST PRO TOURNAMENT WIN

After all her wins and losses were scored by the WITA computer, Steffi began 1986 ranked as the world's No. 6 female tennis player. Her father continued as her coach.

But she still hadn't won the top prize—a singles title—despite playing in 47 professional tournaments. She had won a number of doubles titles, usually teaming with

Gabriela Sabitini of Argentina. In early 1986, she lost to Chris Evert Lloyd in the finals of two tournaments, and to Martina in a semifinal championship.

"Consistency was important in those games with Chris and Martina," she noted.

Computer rankings now moved her to No. 3, right behind Martina and Chris. To be third in the women's tennis world was somewhat overwhelming for 17-year-old Steffi.

"Everything happened a little too fast," said Steffi. "My schedule did not call for me to get this far this fast. I never thought I was going to get to No. 3 so early." She continued her intensive training. She needed to improve her backhand and volley.

In April at the Family Circle Magazine Cup tournament in South Carolina, Steffi faced Chris Evert Lloyd, the No. 2 women's tennis player. Chris had been the winner for eight years.

Chris knew Steffi was a tough opponent. "I always go into a match against Steffi knowing how well she can play," she said before the game. "Steffi's definitely dangerous, and if I play less than well, she's very capable of beating me."

Steffi swiftly devastated Chris, 6-4, 7-5. On reflection she said, "Chris seemed to have a lot of pressure on her, which I didn't have. She just didn't play that well. Now I know I always have a chance against the top players. That's the difference."

Still, winning brings pressures. "I was so nervous," said Steffi. "I'd never made a winner's speech before!"

Questions, questions—reporters want to know all about this talented new tennis star.

Steffi in action during the 1987 U.S. Open.

SOME LOSSES, SOME WINS

In early June 1986, Steffi headed for the French Open. At this point, she had won 24 consecutive matches. Her dream was to reach No. 1 in women's tennis within the next three years. The French Open was a great place to start!

Many believed that Steffi was capable of winning this important tournament. Chris Evert Lloyd said, "She's determined, tough to beat, and has the right mental attitude. I've said all along that Steffi has the game to contend for No. 1."

But Steffi lost in the quarterfinals. She also came down with the flu during the tournament, and was too sick to play at Wimbledon that summer.

Steffi next played at the U.S. Open, held in early fall in New York. She played outstanding tennis in the semifinals against Martina. However, near the end of the tiebreaker, she dropped her racquet while serving. Whatever caused Steffi to falter, Martina seized the opportunity and quickly won.

After the match, Steffi said, "I have to improve my serve much more, and then I think it's going to be a much tougher match for Martina."

Back in New York in late November, she advanced to the finals of the Virginia Slims Championships, held at the Madison Square Garden's Supreme Court. Although she played well, Martina won.

By the end of 1986, at age 17, Steffi was still ranked No. 3. She had won eight singles titles that year, more than all other players, except for Martina. She had played in 14 tournaments. For her outstanding talents, fellow West Germans honored Steffi with the 1986 National Athlete Award.

Once again, her father required Steffi to rest from late November to mid-January 1987. She relaxed, but also worked on her serve and backhand.

NO. 2 IN THE WORLD

In March 1987, Steffi flew to Key Biscayne, Florida, to compete in the Lipton International Players Championship. During the semifinals, she quickly beat top-ranked Martina in 57 minutes, 6-3, 6-2. She took 58 minutes to defeat Chris in the finals, 6-1, 6-2.

After the tournament, Martina said, "Today she was the best player in the world. And she will be until I play her again."

Steffi earned several records with this championship. She became the first to beat Martina and Chris in back-to-back matches, and the third player in the 1980's to defeat both Martina and Chris in the same tournament. She had won two of her last four battles with Martina. She became the fourth player to hold Chris to three games or less in a match.

"I used to say when I played her, that she's got a bright future," said Chris afterwards. "Now I have to say she has

Steffi hits a strong backhand shot.

a great present, past, and future. The men I practice with don't hit that hard. I don't see any reason why she can't win all the tournaments."

"To beat Martina and Chris in three days is very exciting for me," explained Steffi. "When I was growing up, all I saw were Martina and Chris. It's exciting just to stand next to them. I was never too sure I could beat them, but when I play them now I think about winning."

With this victory, Steffi soared past Chris in the rankings. Steffi was No. 2 in the world!

DEFENDING A TITLE

When Steffi returned to South Carolina to compete in the Family Circle Magazine Cup, she was under pressure to defend her first-ever pro title.

Steffi did not concentrate well during her matches, but still won. Her most difficult game was the semifinals against her doubles partner, Gabriela Sabatini. When Steffi made a careless play, Gabriela tried to seize the advantage. Steffi gave herself a mental scolding and took control.

"I told myself, 'It's time to wake up right now,' " she remembered. " 'You can't play like this anymore and expect to win.' " She won and advanced to the finals.

She successfully defended her title, winning the finals against another young player, Manuela Maleeva. She was awarded nearly $60,000 for the singles title. With this check, Steffi had now earned over $1 million during her five-year professional career.

After only five years in professional tennis, Steffi was ranked No. 2!

Concentrating on the next shot.

Opponents brace themselves when Steffi uses her powerful forehand.

EUROPEAN VICTORIES

During May 1987, Steffi won her fifth consecutive tournament, the Italian Open. Steffi reached the finals with a 6-3, 6-3 victory. "That was my best match of the tournament," she later exclaimed.

Steffi now had 27 wins out of 27 matches. But she still was ranked No. 2. Because the rankings are computed over 52 weeks, four great months didn't necessarily mean a No. 1 ranking for Steffi.

Steffi understood the system. "Martina will still be No. 1 after this tournament. She's on top and I'm No. 2. The rankings speak clearly. What more can I say?"

Martina declared, "Steffi's been the best so far this year. Based on the past twelve months, I'm No. 1. But Steffi's one of the reasons I work so hard!"

FIRST GRAND SLAM WIN

The French Open, held in June in Paris, is the world's unofficial clay-court championship. It's highly rated in popularity and importance.

To win the French Open would mean a lot to Steffi, because she would earn her first Grand Slam (a Grand Slam is winning four major international championships in a row).

Steffi entered the championship with 32 straight wins and as the winner of all of her six 1987 tournaments. Her finals opponent, Martina, had not won a tournament for eight months. Also, Martina found clay courts difficult.

That Saturday, Steffi became the youngest women's French Open winner by beating Martina in a magnificent 6-4, 4-6, 8-6 final. Martina shook her head. "Steffi never missed a shot when she was down."

Explained Steffi, "Against Martina, I didn't feel like I could win, so I just decided to go for my shots. I didn't think we'd have such a close match again. It was like the U.S. Open."

Steffi became the second youngest Grand Slam winner

Steffi proudly shows off the winner's trophy for the 1987 French Open.

in history. "The French Open will always be the biggest," she exclaimed. "This will always be the most special for me because it's my first Grand Slam. I've always thought of winning this tournament, but never thought I'd win it at 17."

The second youngest Grand Slam winner is ready for another game.

906088

"Ben" and "Max" are always happy to see Steffi.

A SPECIAL BIRTHDAY

With her prize money from the French Open, Steffi had earned $567,000 by mid-1987. With such money she could afford to buy several sports cars, but she couldn't legally

drive in her own country. But when she turned 18 on June 14, 1987, she could finally get her German driver's license, sign her checks, and vote.

Otherwise, her life stayed pretty much the same. Her daily routine did not change. She usually wakes up by 7:30

a.m., practices at least four hours every day, plays matches, and goes to sleep by 9:30 p.m.

Her life is not all tennis. She collects T-shirts, shorts, leather jackets, and miniature bottles. She loves animals, and has a huge collection of stuffed animals, especially teddy bears. Usually her two dogs, Ben and Max, tag along when she goes jogging, cycling, or swimming. Ben is a boxer, and Max is a German shepherd. She loves music and buys lots of cassette tapes.

But part of Steffi's life has changed. She is a superstar not

Every day more and more fan mail is delivered to the Graf's home.

only in Germany but around the world. She is instantly recognized wherever she travels. "When I go to the shopping malls, people stop and talk to me and ask for my autograph. That never happened before," she said.

She also personally answers all her fan mail. Every day, more than 100 letters arrive. "It takes a lot of time, but my mother helps me with some of the requests for pictures," she said. The Grafs have three separate telephone lines to handle her more than 150 weekly calls from fans and the media.

Although Steffi's life has changed, nothing will take away her love for tennis.

Another winner's speech by Steffi Graf!

1987 WIMBLEDON

Steffi missed last year's Wimbledon tournament due to flu, but reached the fourth round in both 1984 and 1985. With her exciting 1987 wins, experts eagerly awaited her performance on Wimbledon's grass. Most players look at Wimbledon as the top tennis event.

Steffi, however, had more experience playing on her favorite surfaces, hard or clay courts. "It will be very difficult for me at Wimbledon," she admitted. Steffi hadn't played on grass for two years, and grass courts require a different playing style. Steffi was the first player in history to enter Wimbledon unbeaten for the calendar year.

Steffi felt relaxed. "I don't think there is any pressure on me. If you always win, how can there be pressure?"

At least one worried opponent plotted her game strategy against Steffi. "Steffi Graf," declared Martina, "is playing closer to her potential than anyone out here. I have to go flat out, risk everything, or I might as well give up right now."

To keep her winning streak intact before the Wimbledon tournament, Steffi decided to remain in London and practice on grass courts. She didn't play at either of the 1987 grass warm-up tournaments.

At the Wimbledon quarterfinals, she defeated her teenage rival, Gabriela. She won the semifinals 6-1, 6-2, over Pam Shriver. Now she faced Martina in the finals.

Martina won 7-5, 6-3. She defeated Steffi by serving often to Steffi's weaker backhand, staying far away from

Steffi prefers to play on clay courts and had to prepare herself for Wimbledon's grass courts.

38

Steffi battles against Martina Navratilova.

her powerful forehand. "I do the same to my opponents," Steffi later said. "I always play to their weakness."

Steffi was proud of her performance, and held the runner-up trophy high in front of the Royal Box.

"As I haven't played on grass for so long," she said, "I think it's unbelievable that I came to the finals the way I did. I feel very happy about it. I just need a little bit more time."

Steffi displays her powerful serve at the 1987 U.S. Open.

Agreeing with her statements, the Duchess of Kent declared, after Steffi bowed, "Not this year, but you'll have your time."

NO. 1!

Steffi finally attained a goal she worked for all her life. She was ranked No. 1 in the world in August 1987!

Then came the U.S. Open where Steffi again met Martina. And, again, Martina beat Steffi in three straight sets.

"I think everything was not working like it usually does," said Steffi after the game. "I was hitting my forehand too late. It wasn't the best timing I could have had."

Despite the loss, Steffi's opponents still admire her talent.

Chris said, "She's fearless and will play the same game whether she is winning or losing."

"Her head is square on her shoulders," said Martina. "She is a fighter. Steffi won't throw in the towel and that's a pretty good mark of how far she can go."

Steffi's game has many strengths. Her biggest weapon is her powerful forehand. Steffi has "the best forehand I've ever seen," said Billie Jean King. "It's lethal."

Once on the court, Steffi sticks to business. "I'm all concentration then. I always am really tough on myself and I want the best for myself," said Steffi.

Concentration, determination, and good strokes will carry a player far, but Steffi has other natural gifts. "The only factor I thought might get in her way was if she didn't grow or fill out," said King. "Steffi's now a sturdy 5'9" and 110 pounds."

Steffi loves the game and loves winning. She's also content with her life. "As a tennis player and as a person, I am very happy."

Steffi is a fighter and won't give up her game.

The Graf family is proud of Steffi.

"Tennis and becoming No. 1," she continued, "are not the most important things in my life—health, happiness, and my family are most important."

Steffi will continue to practice and play hard so she can hold on to her No. 1 ranking. The tennis world has seen only the beginning of Steffi's talent!

Taking a break from tennis to pose in front of the hometown sign.

STEFFI GRAF'S PROFESSIONAL STATISTICS

Year	Major Wins
1981	German Juniors 14 and Under
	Orange Bowl 12's
1982	European 12 and Under
	German Juniors 18 and Under
	European 14 and Under
	European Circuit Masters
1984	1984 Summer Olympic Games (women's gold medalist)
1986	Family Circle Magazine Cup
	Sunkist WTA Championship
	U.S. Clay Court Championships (singles and doubles)
	German Open (singles and doubles)
	United Jersey Bank Classic
	Pan Pacific Open (singles and doubles)
	European Women's Indoor (singles and doubles)
	Pretty Polly Classic (singles and doubles)
1987	Virginia Slims of Florida
	Lipton International Players Championships
	Family Circle Magazine Cup
	WITA Championships (singles and doubles)
	Italian Open
	West German Open
	French Open